To

Wayne Cooper
8911 Rose Rd. S.W.
Tacoma Wash

080813

THE CLIPPER SHIP

Frank Knight

THE CLIPPER SHIP

COLLINS
St James's Place, London

William Collins Sons & Co Ltd
London · Glasgow · Sydney · Auckland
Toronto · Johannesburg

First published 1973
© Text Frank Knight 1973
ISBN 00 192147 9
Set in Monophoto Bembo
Made and Printed in Great Britain by
William Collins Sons & Co Ltd Glasgow

Contents

*

CHAPTER ONE

The Coming of the Clippers

*

In the year 1841 a New York naval architect named John Griffith showed American shipowners a model of a new kind of sailing ship. She was long and narrow, with knife-sharp, raking bows. She had straight, wall-like sides and a tapering, tucked-up stern. Her masts, immensely tall, leaned backwards instead of being dead upright. Her wide-spreading spars were clearly intended to carry a huge amount of sail.

Everything about the new ship, every line of her slender hull, every stick and string of her towering rig, spoke of one thing and one thing only – *speed*.

Now American shipowners liked fast ships. They liked captains who would drive their ships hard, to beat all rivals. Men like the captain of the brig *Alert*, for instance, in Richard Dana's famous book *Two Years Before the Mast*.

"Get up the topmast studding-sail!" roars that captain in a Cape Horn gale. And when the mate objects that this may be dangerous, he retorts, "Get it up! What she can't carry she may drag!"

That had been the American spirit in the War of Independence, when fast little ships were built specially to dodge and outsail British warships. They were called Baltimore clippers, because most of them came from Baltimore and because 'clipper' meant a fast horse, from an old Dutch word *klepper*. John Griffith's model, with its overhanging bow and tall raking masts, reminded some shipowners of those old-time Baltimore clippers. But Griffith's ship was intended to be a big, ocean-going cargo carrier, not a little schooner for coastal work.

7

Before the coming of the clippers: a view of shipping on the Canton River at Whampoa, the East India Company station. East Indiamen like the *Waterloo* (right) dominated the trade.

So most owners who saw the model were horrified. "Nobody could sail her!" they protested. "She will capsize in the first stiff breeze!" Someone said that with her concave bows and swept-up stern she was like a ship turned inside out. Worst of all, they complained, she could never pay her way; for she would need more men to handle all that sail, yet her slender hull would carry less cargo. More men to pay, less cargo to sell. It was absurd!

They liked fast ships, these owners. But they had always been used to full-bodied, rounded ships with bluff bows and square sterns and deep, capacious hulls: ships which, above all, could carry plenty of cargo. Speed was good, but not if it meant sacrificing cargo space.

So they sent John Griffith away, not knowing that within five short years they would be begging him to build them clipper ships on the lines of his model!

*   *   *

If John Griffith had shown his model in Britain he would have been laughed at even more. For British shipowners did not want fast ships at all, because they had practically no competition. Britain was the world's leading sea-trading nation, with an empire extending all over the world and still growing. For hundreds of years no foreign ships had been allowed to trade on any of those empire routes. The ancient Navigation Acts forbade it.

On the most profitable routes of all, those between Britain and India and the Far East, British shipowners were not even allowed to compete among themselves, for these routes were entirely reserved for ships in the service of the mighty East India Company.

These were the finest ships in the world, built and run like battleships, with big crews and whole broadsides of guns. They could fight, too, if they had to. In 1800 one of them captured a French frigate, and in 1804 a fleet of them put to flight a French battle squadron.

The *Renown*, a Blackwall frigate. These ships were faster than the old East Indiamen, but they were not clippers.

The cargoes these ships carried were worth fighting for – silks, spices, tea, perfumes, carpets, precious stones and every kind of luxury. They were worth carrying safely, no matter how slowly, and East India captains never took risks. What did it matter if a voyage to India lasted six months, or a round trip to China and back two whole years? There was no competition – no need to hurry.

But all this was changing. The East India Company, with its own army and navy and its private empire, had grown too powerful. Gradually the British government took steps to bring it to an end. In 1813 trade with India was opened to all comers. Twenty years later, in 1833, trade with China was also thrown open, and in fact 'John Company' was forbidden to operate ships at all, except on the Indian coast.

The *Kent*, a Blackwall frigate of later years with reduced sailing rig
and auxiliary steam power.

That brought competition, and competition brought faster ships. New East Indiamen appeared, built less like battleships and more like frigates. Indeed they were called Blackwall frigates, because most of them were built at Blackwall on the River Thames. They reduced the time for a voyage to India from six months to three, and a round trip to China and back from two years to one. But they were not clippers. Their owners, and all British shipowners, still believed that 'slow but sure' was a better motto than 'speed at any price'.

*   *   *

It was the China tea trade which brought in the true clipper – the ship in which speed mattered above everything.

In those days China was the only country in the world where tea was grown in big quantities. But buying it had always been a difficult business, which had made it very expensive. It was a difficult business because the Chinese detested foreigners and really had no wish to trade with them at all.

The emperor of China believed that he ruled the entire world, and such people as Americans and Europeans were his barbarian subjects. Even Queen Victoria was to him merely a vassal princess – a vassal who lived principally upon tea! As to merchants and ships' captains and the like, they were no better than slaves or beggars.

Foreign ships were allowed into only one Chinese port, Canton, and for only a short while in each year when the tea crop was ready. Nobody from the ships was allowed to go ashore, except a few merchants or their agents, and they were kept practically in prison.

Worst of all, the tea had to be paid for on the spot, in silver. No foreign goods were allowed to be bought by Chinese in exchange. And that infuriated European and American merchants who had goods to sell, especially manufactured goods such as cotton cloth. What a market China would be for that if only the door could be opened!

Unhappily for China a few unscrupulous British and American traders had discovered what amounted to a side door into the forbidden land. They had found that the Chinese had a passion for opium. Its importation into China was forbidden by law, but if it could be smuggled in there were many Chinese merchants and even corrupt government officials ready to pay for it with silver. So very soon a huge illegal traffic in the drug had grown up, with opium produced in India being smuggled into China by fast little ships which came to be known as opium clippers.

They were not the ocean-going clippers which were to come later. They were of all types and rigs. One, the *Falcon*, had been an English nobleman's yacht and flagship of the Royal Yacht Squadron. Their chief importance, from our point of view, was that many of the captains and crews of the later clippers were trained in them.

Opium smuggling, however, was of no use to Lancashire cotton manufacturers who wanted to sell their goods in China.

Opium ships at Lintin in China, 1824. Almost any type of ship involved in the smuggling of opium from India to China was known as an 'opium clipper'.

Tea had been a way of life in the pleasure gardens of Britain for more than a century, but suddenly in the 1840s it seemed that everyone wanted to drink China tea, and the fresher the better. Hence the importance of speed and the beginning of the reign of the clippers.

They pestered the British government to *force* China to open her doors, and at last, in 1839, the government acted, though the excuse taken was a strange one. Chinese officials had burnt a quantity of British-owned opium, so the British government sent warships and troops to punish them! It was called the First Opium War, but most people knew that it was really about ordinary trade, especially in tea and cotton.

The war dragged on for four years, but at last the Chinese gave way. Five ports were opened to foreign trade – Canton, Amoy, Foochow, Ningpo and Shanghai; and Britain was given possession of Hong Kong Island. So now the way was open and shipowners everywhere prepared to take advantage of it. But especially American shipowners. Almost before the ink was dry on the famous treaty, in 1843, a New York firm had asked John Griffith to build them a real clipper like his model.

Why the sudden hurry? Because everyone, in America at any

The Fontenaye was built in 1864 by Moore's of Sunderland and measured 635 tons.

UNLOADING THE TEA-SHIPS.

We have noticed the competition between the owners of fast-sailing vessels employed in the China tea trade for the honour of bringing to the port of London the first cargo that arrives here of the freshly gathered crop of tea, which is always plucked in the spring season. The market in Mincing-lane is very busy in this month of October with the "New Season Teas," both those of China and those of the Himalayan provinces of India, which have latterly found favour. The unloading of the tea-ships and warehousing of their cargoes on the wharves of the East India Docks is also a scene of great activity, as shown in one of our Illustrations.

Picture and caption from the Illustrated London News, October 1867.

Tea manufacture in China. The tea leaves, having been brought in from the gardens and dried (left), are then sorted and sifted (right).

rate, was eager to be first in the field. Because huge profits were expected to be made out of this new trade. Because everybody, it seemed, wanted to drink China tea and would pay a high price for it – especially if it could be rushed to them quickly, for it was believed that tea was spoilt by being long at sea. The fresher the tea, from each new season's crop, the more money people would pay for it.

So now, at last, speed was all-important. Expense did not matter. Almost any risk could be taken. Cargo space could be sacrificed. Nothing mattered except speed!

But British shipowners saw no need to join in the rush. The Navigation Acts were still in force, which forbade foreign ships from entering British ports except when carrying the produce of their own countries. So no American ship, thank goodness, would be allowed to carry tea from China to Britain! Secure against such competition, most British shipowners concluded that 'slow but sure' was still the best policy.

John Griffith's clipper *Rainbow*, the first of all clippers, was launched in January 1845. On her first voyage she broke all records, going out to China and back in seven months. On her second voyage she broke that record by half a month. John Land, her master, declared that no ship could *ever* be built to beat her.

But Captain Land was wrong. John Griffith built a second clipper, *Sea Witch*, and she was even faster. Then other designers tried their hands, and within two or three years a whole fleet of tall American clippers were competing in the China trade.

Then came a fantastic piece of luck for the clipper owners and builders. Gold was discovered in California. Suddenly thousands of people who had scarcely heard of the place before wanted to go there. Some trudged overland, across deserts and mountains and fighting Indians on the prairies. Others, who could afford it, took ship to Panama, crossed the Isthmus by mule train, then took another ship to the golden land. But many more preferred to take one ship all the way, right around the Cape Horn and

Tea packing for export. Gaily coloured wooden tea chests were lined with lead foil, which was lightweight, yet protected the tea from strong odours.

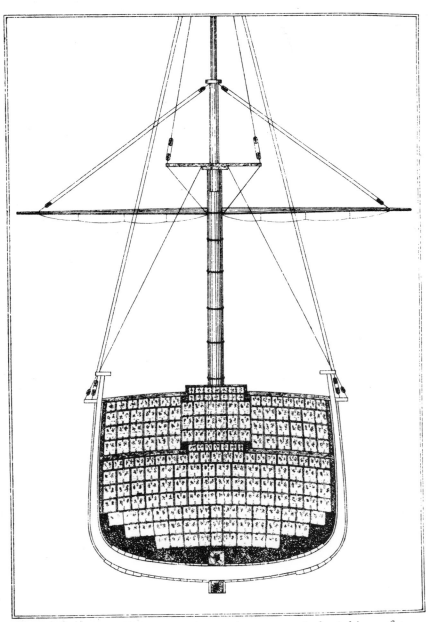

This cross-section of a ship shows the economical packing of tea (from R. W. Stevens' *On the Stowage of Ships and their Cargoes*, 1854).

The *Eliza Nicholson* of 1863. This oil painting shows the vessel with painted ports (rare in the tea trade) and an old-fashioned bow.

northward through the Pacific. And the faster the ship, the higher the fare she could charge.

To meet the rush anything that would float was patched up and sent on its way. Ships were hastily built in fields where no shipyard had existed before. Eight hundred ships battled their way round Cape Horn in the first year of the rush, 1849. Nobody knows how many more set out but never arrived.

For the real clippers it was a golden time indeed. Crammed with eager diggers, and with every kind of goods for the new towns and mining camps, they raced out to California in ninety or a hundred days, then hurried across the Pacific to load China tea. So profitable was this double trade that some ships paid off their entire building cost in one voyage.

And the golden years were even then only just beginning. It was as though nothing could go wrong for the American clippers. First the opening of trade with China, then the Californian gold-rush; and then, in that same year of 1849, Britain abolished the Navigation Acts and opened her ports and trade routes to foreign competition. There were several reasons. One was that some people had at last realized that the protection from competition given by the Navigation Acts was doing more harm than good. It was merely protecting and encouraging the least enterprising kind of shipowner, with the result that British ship-design was falling far behind that of other nations. Another reason was that some nations, including America, were playing 'tit-for-tat' and closing their ports to British ships. Britain, as the greatest sea-trading nation in the world, had far more to lose from such a policy than had her rivals. A third reason, perhaps the most important of all, was that Britain, at this time, was trying to persuade the rest of the world that *free* trade was best for everybody – no import or export duties, no restrictions of any kind. In those circumstances the Navigation Acts *had* to be abolished.

Like hounds on a fresh scent the big clippers leapt into the new trade. Before the end of 1849 the American *Oriental*, of 1,600 tons, had rushed a cargo of China tea to London, easily outsail-

The port of New York in 1849, a great year for American shipping. The California gold rush had begun, and Britain was opening her ports and trade routes to foreign competition.

The early 1850s were golden years indeed for the real American clippers. The *Donald Mackay* (above) was bought by a British ship-owner, James Baines, for the Australian trade and the *Swiftsure* (below) was chartered by an English firm during the Gold Rush.

ing the slower British ships and throwing British owners into a state of panic. And she was followed by many others.

Yet even that was not the end of the amazing boom. In 1851 gold was discovered in Australia also, and a second frantic rush began. And yet again the big American clippers were there to make the fastest passages and take the cream of the trade, though this time some of them sailed under the British flag. One British owner, the fiery little James Baines of Liverpool, had discovered an American clipper builder of genius, the great Donald Mackay of Boston, and had ordered four ships from him. These four, *Lightning*, *Champion of the Seas*, *James Baines* and *Donald Mackay*, all of about 2,500 tons, were the queens of the Australian passenger trade during the 1850s. Some of the records they set up have never yet been beaten, especially a marvellous run by the *Champion of the Seas* of 465 nautical miles in one day.

*　　*　　*

Thus in less than ten years American clippers had become supreme on almost every ocean route. Yet in less than ten years more they would practically have vanished from the scene.

In 1853, the peak year, no fewer than fifty new clippers came from American yards. Four years later only three were built, and after that scarcely any. For most of the 1850s they dominated the China tea trade. But by 1860 they had almost all gone from it. Even in San Francisco, once crowded with the tall Cape Horn conquerors, there were more foreign ships than American, and hardly a true clipper amongst them.

Why did this happen, and so swiftly? There were many reasons. Just as the strokes of good fortune had crowded into a few years, so now the setbacks seemed to come all together.

These big clippers were very expensive to build and to run. They needed big crews, and good seamen were hard to find. Their sails, spars and rigging wore out at a fantastic rate. Their wooden hulls, always driven hard, soon developed leaks so that their cargoes were spoilt. Many were lost at sea. All of which sent insurance rates up and up, which added to the

J. P. Whitney, a typical example of a straight-sided American clipper of the 1850s, with enormous single (undivided) topsails.

expense. And, to make matters worse, their timbers soon became saturated with water, which made them heavy and sluggish. Almost all American clippers were past their best after four or five years.

None of this mattered much while profits were high. But after about 1856 profits began to decline. Gold-rush fever had died down. More ships every year were competing for the steady trade which remained. In the tea trade British, French and Swedish ships were competing, and the British tea clippers, in particular, were showing themselves a match for the Americans. Moreover these older shipping nations seemed to be able to run ships far more cheaply than could the Americans.

Then there were steamships, which once had been treated with scorn by sailing-ship men. But every year they were becoming bigger, more reliable, and faster. They had already beaten sailing clippers in the North Atlantic passenger trade, and soon no doubt would conquer on other routes. And there were railways spreading all across America, taking goods and passengers which had once travelled by sea. Soon, almost for certain, they would link the Atlantic with the Pacific overland, and that would completely kill the Cape Horn route to California.

Americans, including shipowners, began to turn away from the sea and look towards their vast land. It offered so many

Blue Jacket, another big American-built clipper which became famous on the Australian run under the British flag. She caught fire and was abandoned near the Falkland Islands in 1869. Nearly two years later her figurehead was washed ashore on the coast of Western Australia.

The Confederate warship *Alabama* captured 65 Northern ships in two years; and the Civil War brought an end to the Yankee clipper's brief but spectacular dominance of the seas.

opportunities – farming, mining, cutting down forests, building new towns and more railways. Why bother about the sea?

All this came about just when many clippers were becoming old and obsolete and should have been replaced with new ones. Instead of replacing them, owners either went in for steamers, or gave up shipowning altogether.

And finally came political troubles. Quarrelling between the northern and southern states broke into civil war in 1861. Each side raided the other's shipping, so that no American vessel was safe and cargo owners would only ship their goods in foreign hulls. One Southern warship, the famous *Alabama*, captured sixty-five Northern ships in two years, and sent scores of others

The *Min* in a rough sea. The main sail and mizzen sail have been taken in against the coming storm. Built in 1861 as a tea clipper, she was finally sold to the Hawaiians and sailed the Pacific island trade under several other names.

scurrying into harbour, never to put to sea again. America's shipping industry lay in ruins, and was not to recover for half a century.

* * *

British shipowners scarcely gave clippers a thought until the *Oriental* and others like her captured the tea trade. And when that happened many of them could only throw up their hands in despair and plead with the government to bring back the old Navigation Acts.

Fortunately the government refused to do any such thing, and more enterprising owners set themselves to meet the American onslaught. "At last we have sat down to play a fair and open game with the Americans," exclaimed one of them, Richard Green of Blackwall, "and, by God, we'll trump them!"

In 1852 Britain's first real clipper, the *Challenger*, raced the U.S. clipper *Challenge* and won. The legend is that her owner won so much money in bets on this contest that he bought the American ship (shown below) with his winnings. Britain was finally in the clipper race.

Richard Green had so far built only Blackwall frigates, but now he set about designing a clipper, which in due course he named *Challenger*. Loading tea for the first time in 1852, she raced an American clipper named *Challenge* home, beat her by two days, and made so much money in bets for Richard Green that – so the story goes – he bought the American ship with his winnings!

Other shipowners, without their own building yards, had to look around for a builder enterprising enough to try his hand at a clipper. Few British builders had any experience of building fast ships of any kind. But they found the man they wanted in the little Scottish port of Aberdeen – Alexander Hall. For years he had been building speedy little ships for the coastal passenger trade. Could he build bigger ships on the same lines? He could, and he did. In 1851 the very first genuine British clippers left his yard, *Stornoway* and *Chrysolite*.

True, they were only half the size of the big American clippers, but that made them more suitable for the tricky waters of the China Sea. This was demonstrated on the *Chrysolite's* first voyage, when she took a short cut between two reefs. An American ship, the *Memnon*, tried to follow her, struck one of the reefs, and was lost.

Other British clippers came from the yards as more owners and builders took courage to try their hands. Beautiful ships with beautiful names – *Crest of the Wave*, *Spirit of the Age*, *Cairngorm*, *Lord of the Isles*, *Fiery Cross*, *Robin Hood*. Racing between British and American ships became intense. Prizes were offered to captains and extra pay to winning crews. People who had scarcely seen a ship before used to bet on the results of each year's tea race.

When in 1860 the Americans dropped out, British clippers continued the racing among themselves. More ships joined in – *Highflyer*, *Star of China*, *Taeping*, *Wild Deer*, *Golden Spur*, *Ariel*, *Sir Lancelot* and many others, to be outdone at last by the two fastest of them all, *Thermopylae* and *Cutty Sark*.

And then came the end. In 1869 the Suez Canal was opened.

It shortened all routes to the East by thousands of miles, but it was a route for steamers, not sailing ships. It led through the Mediterranean Sea into the Red Sea, where sailing ships would find fickle winds and frustrating calms. Moreover sailing ships would have to be towed through the Canal itself by an expensive steam tug.

Gone were the days when the crew of a clipper would dangle a rope over the stern as their ship overtook a steamer, jeeringly offering the puffing 'kettle' a tow. Now the despised steamers could make the voyage home from China in fifty days or so, while the best of the racing clippers could seldom do it in less than a hundred. Now even wonder-ships like *Thermopylae* and *Cutty Sark* could not get a cargo of tea in China if there were a steamer to take it instead.

So the clippers went into other trades. Some, like *Thermopylae* and *Cutty Sark*, for a few years found a use for their speed in rushing the Australian wool-clip home each season. But in most trades all-out speed was not wanted. What was required was cheapness. A sailing ship might still get cargoes if she could carry them more cheaply than steamers, but not otherwise.

For the sake of economy, then, the tall clippers had their rigs cut down, their crews reduced, their sails and spars patched instead of being renewed. The era of the true clipper had gone for ever.

CHAPTER TWO

The Building of the Clippers

*

ALL American clippers and most British ones were built of wood. Two or three British clippers were built of wrought iron – not steel, because no means of producing steel in big quantities, cheaply, was invented until the 1870s.

Iron was not popular for clippers because it was heavy,

Crest of the Wave, one of the beautiful British clippers built in 1853.

In the 1860s the Aberdeen firm of Duthies launched several wool clippers, all named after members of the family. This one is the *Ann Duthie*.

expensive, and too rigid. Sailing ships, said the experts, must be flexible – must be allowed to *work*, to use a technical term. It was also thought that iron would sweat, and so damage the cargo. The experts did not change their minds even though the iron clipper *Lord of the Isles*, built in 1853, proved herself as fast as any then afloat and always delivered her tea in perfect condition. No other iron clipper was built till 1870, at the very end of the clipper-ship era.

British clipper builders invented a compromise, however. Most of the British tea clippers of the 1860s were planked with wood upon a framework, or skeleton, of iron. This was called

WILLIAM LIGERTWOOD (BOATBUILDER)   GEO. SIM (CARPENTER)   JOHN HADDEN (BLOCKMAKER)   JAMES MORRISON (BLACKSMITH)   WILLIAM SHEARER (CASHIER)   PETER ANDERSON (FOREMAN JOINER)

JAS CARNIE (FOREMAN CARPENTER)   ALEX. GUYAN (GATE KEEPER)

ALEX H WILSON (SHIPBUILDER)   ROBT. ROBERTSON (BLACKSMITH)   WILLIAM HALL JNR. JOHN GUNN (FOREMAN CARPENTER)

JAMES SHAND (FOREMAN CARPENTER)   WALTER DINNET (FOREMAN CARPENTER)   JAMES MITCHELL (FOREMAN CARPENTER)   JAMES ANDERSON J (CARPENTER)

The designers and builders of the Aberdeen clippers,
Alexander Hall and Sons.

JOHN
CRUICKSHANK
(OFFICE. BOY)

ROBERT
CROLL
(OFFICE)

'composite' building and was highly successful. Some American clippers had iron 'knees' or brackets to strengthen their framework, but in America the full composite system was not generally used.

In America wood was cheap and plentiful. In many places great forests extended almost to the shore line and timber was to be had for the cutting. But most of it was 'soft' – pine, larch, and inferior kinds of oak. In the rush to build ships quickly it was often used 'green', or unseasoned. Because of that it was inclined to warp, twist and shrink after the ship was built.

It used to be said that some ships 'worked' so much – opened and closed big gaps between their timbers as they strained in a rough sea – that it was dangerous for a man to sit down on deck, for his trousers or even his skin might be nipped between two planks!

Most British tea clippers, on the other hand, were built of imported 'hard' woods – teak, mahogany and the like. This, with their iron framing, made them costly. But they seldom leaked, and sailors used to say they were 'as tight as bottles'.

American ships were built of softwood and eventually became sodden and sluggish, but the British ships had longer lives because they were built of hardwood. A fine example is the *Cutty Sark*, shown here under sail and, right, preserved at Greenwich.

The giant American ship *Great Republic* was the only clipper to have four masts rather than three, as shown in this very early photograph of 1853.

Nor did they become sodden and sluggish like the soft-wood American clippers, so that they remained serviceable and fast for many years. The Aberdeen White Star Line kept the *Thermopylae* on their Australian run till 1890, and after that she served as a training ship for the Portuguese navy till 1907. John Willis, first owner of the *Cutty Sark*, did not sell her till 1895, but she was still good enough to work as a cargo-carrier under the Portuguese flag till 1921, when she was brought back to Britain to be restored to her original form and preserved as a memorial to the past.

*   *   *

Normally clippers had three masts, fore-, main- and mizzen-, setting square-sails on each. In other words they were 'ship' rigged. Only one clipper had four masts, Donald Mackay's giant *Great Republic* of 4,500 tons, built in 1853, but she was not as successful as his smaller ships.

Each mast comprised three sections – lower mast, topmast, and topgallant mast. The upper half of the topgallant mast might be called the royal mast. Both top- and topgallant masts could be lowered to the deck if required, but it was a complicated job, not to be done at sea if it could be avoided.

On the lower masts would be set the fore-, main- and mizzen yards, the last named also being called the crossjack or cro'jack yard. The main yard, hoisted to about fifty feet above the deck, might be sixty or eighty feet long and thick enough for a man to walk along.

The topmasts carried the topsail yards, the topgallant masts, both topgallant and royal yards and perhaps skysail yards above those. Some of the biggest clippers even carried 'moon-raker' yards above the skysails.

The total height of the mainmast in *Cutty Sark* was 146 feet. In the *Great Republic*, the biggest clipper ever built, it was 226 feet. Working on a slender yard at such a height, especially in a breeze was no joke!

All rigging was of hemp or cotton rope. Wire rope was not used until much later, after most clippers had vanished. Nylon and other man-made fibres had of course not been invented, though nylon rope has been used in re-rigging *Cutty Sark* in her permanent drydock. In a clipper ship there might be as many as two hundred separate ropes, each with its special purpose – for supporting the masts, supporting and trimming the yards, hoisting and trimming sails and so on. Their names formed part of the sea-language which every sailor was expected to know – stays, hoists, downhauls and outhauls, clewlines, buntlines and gaskets, sheets, vangs, footropes, strops, ratlines and shrouds. Every sailor had to know what each one did and where it could found even in darkness. None was labelled!

Sails were made of flax or cotton canvas. American ships were often distinguishable by the whiteness of their cotton sails; but cotton was thicker and stiffer and more difficult to handle than flax. Sails could be set and trimmed from the deck, but furling and reefing had to be done aloft, by men working on the yards.

The clipper *Spindrift*, winner of the 1868 tea race from China. Right: a scale model showing the ship's rigging. Left: a drawing showing the sail plan.

Imagine leaning over a yard, scores of feet above the deck, with one's feet treading only a swaying footrope, grabbing and clawing at a mass of billowing canvas, probably wet and possibly stiff with ice, while the ship leaps and swerves below and the world seems to have gone mad about one. This was when muscles were strained, hands gashed and fingernails torn away; and when, all too often, men lost their hold and went overboard. A man lost overboard from a sailing ship in such conditions could not hope to be picked up.

In the 'ship' rig used by the clippers the lowest and biggest sail on each mast was called the 'course' – foresail or forecourse, mainsail or main-course, mizzen course or cro'jack. Above the courses were the topsails – single topsails in the older ships, but divided for ease of handling into upper and lower topsails in later vessels. Next came the topgallants, also divided into upper and lower sails in the later ships. Above them the royals, and then skysails and possibly moonrakers.

But these were only the squaresails, set across the ship.

One of the American clippers that sailed to Australia in the 1850s under the *James Baines*, built by Donald Mackay of Boston.

There were also the fore-and-aft sails, set in the fore-and-aft line of the vessel, on the stays supporting the masts.

Set on the foremast-stays, leading down to the bowsprit and jibboom, would be the fore-topmast staysail, then inner-, outer- and flying jibs. Other staysails would be set between the fore- and mainmasts, and between the main- and mizzen masts. Abaft the mizzen mast would be the spanker, shaped like a cutter's mainsail, spread by its boom and gaff. This might also be called the 'driver'.

These were the normal working sails. In suitable weather others would be set, such as studding-sails or stunsails outside and extending the width of the lower squaresails. There might be 'watersails' hanging beneath the lowest stunsails almost down to the surface of the sea. There might be extra sails on the bowsprit and jibboom, and 'bonnets' laced in to fill gaps between sails, and a triangular topsail above the spanker. Some captains invented strange sails of their own. The sailors of the *Thermopylae* once even spread their blankets in the rigging to give their ship a little more urge against a rival!

Even without such extras, a clipper might set nearly an acre of canvas. *Cutty Sark*'s normal sail plan measured 32,000 square feet. A new suit of sails for her would require *four miles* of canvas of 24-inches width. It has been calculated that the sails of a clipper, in a good breeze, would generate 3,000 horsepower. But for a really big clipper like the *Great Republic* all these figures might well be doubled.

CHAPTER THREE

Sailing the Clippers

*

BECAUSE of her slender hull and towering sail plan the clipper was much more delicate to handle than any other sailing ship. And every clipper was different from every other one. Each had her own foibles, tricks and mannerisms, which her captain had to study and learn. Most clippers did better on their second and later voyages than on their first, because on the first voyage the captain would only be learning his new ship's ways.

In those days there was more art in designing a ship than science. Naval architects gave a ship the shape which their experience and their artistic sense indicated was right. There were no elaborate testing tanks, as there are today, in which models could be tried out and such things as wave-resistance, windage and rudder effect scientifically measured. Nobody knew for certain how a ship would behave until she put to sea. Every clipper was to some extent an experiment. The astonishing thing is that so few were failures, which proves the skill, amounting to genius, of such designers as John Griffith, Donald Mackay and Alexander Hall.

Most American clippers liked lots of wind and hard driving. They were designed for crossing oceans and for battling round Cape Horn. The smaller British tea clippers, on the other hand, preferred more moderate winds, and could ghost along in the lightest breeze while a heavier ship would be lying stopped.

Some of the early British clippers, including *Stornoway* and *Chrysolite*, would show their disapproval of hard driving by digging their bows into the sea and possibly washing men off the jibboom. But some of the later ones, like *Sir Lancelot* and *Ariel*

43

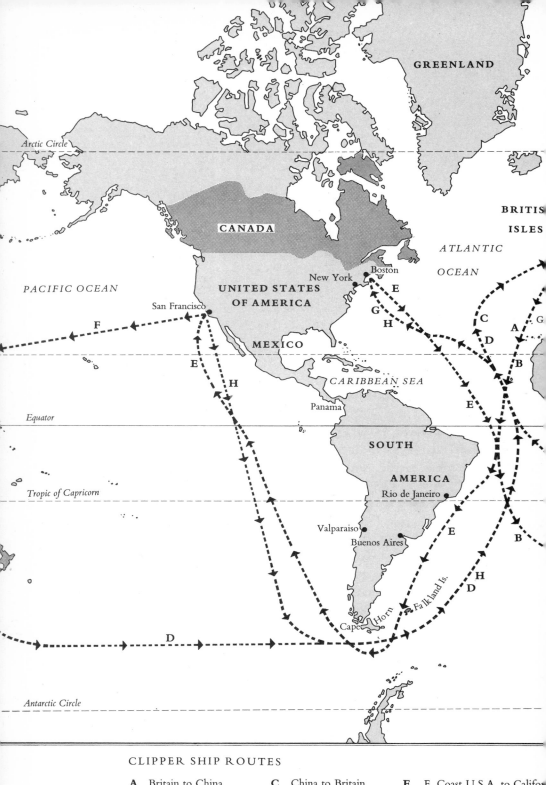

GREENLAND

Arctic Circle

BRITISH

ISLES

ATLANTIC

CANADA

OCEAN

Boston
New York
E

UNITED STATES
OF AMERICA

G

C

G

PACIFIC OCEAN

San Francisco

F

H

A

MEXICO

D

E

B

CARIBBEAN SEA

E

H

Panama

Equator

SOUTH

AMERICA

Tropic of Capricorn

Rio de Janeiro

E

Valparaiso

B

Buenos Aires

E

Falkland Is.

H

D

D

Cape Horn

Antarctic Circle

CLIPPER SHIP ROUTES

A Britain to China   **C** China to Britain   **E** E. Coast U.S.A. to Califor

B Britain to Australia   **D** Australia to Britain   **F** California to China

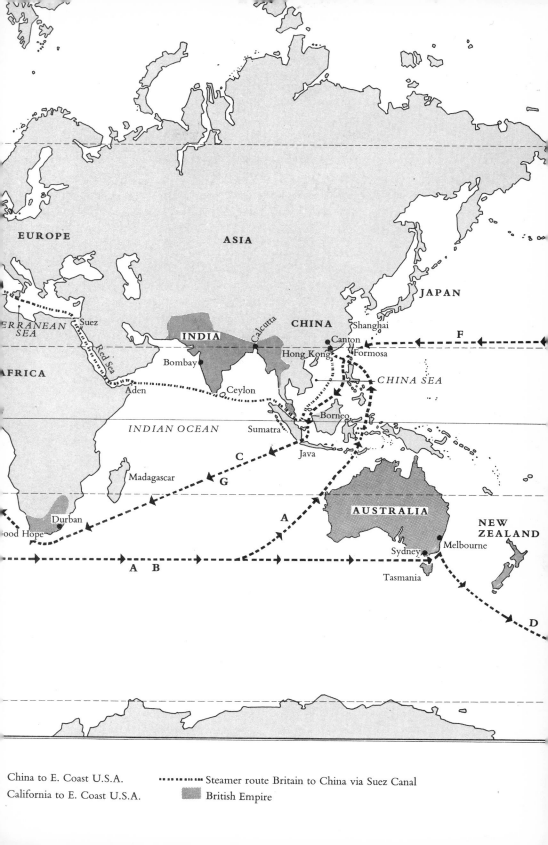

EUROPE ASIA

JAPAN

MEDITERRANEAN SEA Suez

CHINA Shanghai

INDIA Calcutta Canton Formosa

Bombay Hong Kong

AFRICA *Red Sea*

Aden Ceylon F

CHINA SEA

INDIAN OCEAN Borneo

Sumatra C

Java G

Madagascar

Durban A

...ood Hope AUSTRALIA NEW ZEALAND

A B Sydney Melbourne

Tasmania D

China to E. Coast U.S.A. ••••••••••• Steamer route Britain to China via Suez Canal

California to E. Coast U.S.A. [British Empire shading] British Empire

would act in the opposite way, sitting down on their sterns and letting the sea come pouring in over the poop, perhaps washing men away from the wheel or even smashing the wheel.

They were all different. Some were at their best with a following wind, some with the wind abeam, some when beating against a head wind. Some could be tacked to and fro on short zig-zag courses, so that they would sail virtually against the wind up a river. But others would refuse to swing from one tack to the other, and would rush astern as soon as the wind drew ahead.

The tea clipper *Titania* was one which loved going astern, but on one occasion she was coaxed all the way up the Yangtse-Kiang to Shanghai by letting her make one crossing of the river forwards, then one astern, then another ahead, and so on until she reached the port. In such ways a skilful captain, thoroughly knowing his ship, could make use even of her little awkwardnesses. There were few steam tugs in distant ports in those days and the clippers often had to be sailed right up to their moorings or loading berths.

This was not easy. It required all the captain's skill in knowing precisely when and how to trim his sails or move his rudder. And every command he gave must be obeyed instantly, for a clipper had a will of her own and would take advantage of every hesitation, every mistake. So two men would be at the wheel straining their muscles. And everyone else, often including the cook and cabin boy, would be pulling and hauling and swearing as the mates drove them on.

It was upon how he drove or coaxed his ship along the ocean routes, however, and upon how he chose those routes, that a clipper captain's success or failure depended. Whether to take a northerly or a southern line, whether to go east or west of an island, whether to hug a coastline or keep well out at sea, whether to hold to the shortest possible track or to go miles out of the way to look for a fair wind.

As with the ship-designer, he had little scientific aid. There were no weather reports, no radio warnings. He had his

On the rigging. Frayed ropes had to be repaired and wire stays greased. The sails and rigging of a sailing ship were, in a sense, her 'engine' and had to be kept in efficient running order.

barometer and what signs he might read from the clouds. He had his own past experience and some experiences of other men. He had some knowledge of the prevailing winds of the world.

When Christopher Columbus first crossed to America he found a strong and steady wind from the northeast which carried his ships almost all the way from Spain to the West Indies. He found it again on his second voyage. But he still failed to realize how permanent it was, and on his third voyage went much further to the south, so missing this Trade Wind – as we call it now – and becoming becalmed and frustrated in the area we call the Doldrums.

A few years later Magellan found a similar constant wind in the Pacific, the Southeast Trade Wind. Other navigators followed his route to the East Indies, using the same wind. But for forty years nobody could find a way back from the East Indies to America, except by beating all the way against this trade wind, which in the ships of those days was practically impossible. Not until 1565 did a man named Urdaneta explore far to the northward and discover in latitude 40°N. a similar wind, blowing from the west. We call it the Anti-Trade, but to those early Spanish navigators it was such a discovery that for a century this route was known as Urdaneta's Passage.

In such ways, slowly and sometimes painfully, knowledge was gathered. But unfortunately it was not passed on. Captains kept their secrets, hoping thereby to make themselves more important. Nations locked away and guarded log-books, charts and reports in case any rival nation should score over them. Columbus infuriated King John of Portugal because he would not tell his 'secrets' to him. England and Spain almost went to war over an argument as to which country was to have the services of Sebastian Cabot, with his private knowledge of winds and seaways.

Then, just as the clippers were coming into existence in the 1840s, all that was at last altered, largely by the efforts of one man, Lieutenant Matthew Maury of the United States Navy.

Maury had been a keen navigator for years, and during a

The *Ellen Rodger* was a fast little ship that did long service in the tea trade. Like many another of her kind she was finally wrecked off the China coast.

four-year cruise round the world had studied winds and currents and similar matters. But in 1839 an accident put an end to his sea-going career. In 1841 he persuaded the government to let him work ashore at the business of gathering and sorting out information about the oceans.

He studied thousands of log-books, issued forms for ships' officers to complete, collected information from all over the world, and finally persuaded many governments to meet at a great conference in Brussels. There at last the ancient barriers were broken down and the study of winds, currents and weather became an international matter. In future all navigators, under every flag, would have access to whatever information was available.

*　　　*　　　*

One result of Maury's work was that sailing directions were published in many languages to advise captains as to the best routes to take throughout the world. These were based primarily upon certain wind systems which exist in all the great oceans.

Four of the oceans, North and South Atlantic, North and South Pacific, have similar systems. In each there is a central zone of relatively high barometric pressure around which the wind tends to circulate. In the northern hemisphere this circulation is clockwise, in the southern hemisphere it is anti-clockwise.

The result in practice is that on the equatorial side of each system we have normally strong and steady winds blowing towards the west but inclining towards the Equator – in other words *from* the northeast in the northern oceans, *from* the southeast in the southern oceans. And winds are always named by the direction *from* which they blow.

These are the Trade Winds, so called from an ancient word meaning path or *tread*. They literally marked out the sea-paths for sailing ships, and trade in our modern sense grew along them.

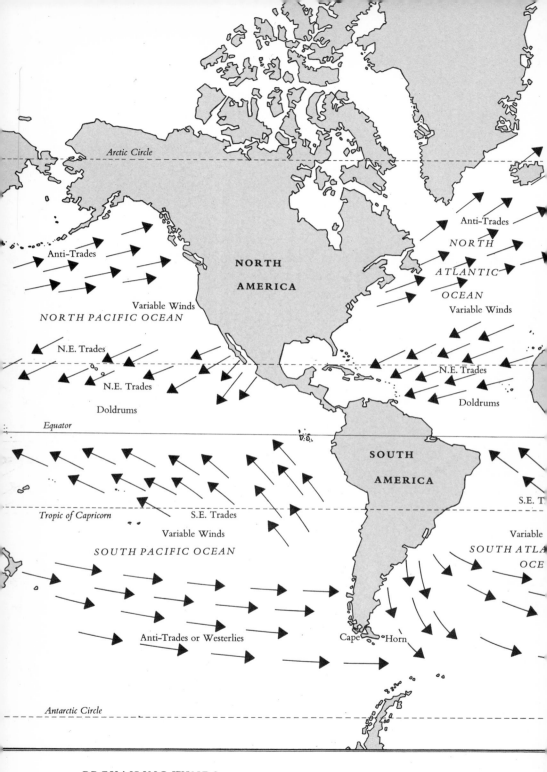

Arctic Circle

Anti-Trades

NORTH
AMERICA

Variable Winds

NORTH PACIFIC OCEAN

N.E. Trades

N.E. Trades

Doldrums

Equator

Anti-Trades

NORTH

ATLANTIC

OCEAN

Variable Winds

N.E. Trades

Doldrums

SOUTH
AMERICA

S.E. T

Tropic of Capricorn   S.E. Trades

Variable Winds

SOUTH PACIFIC OCEAN

Variable

SOUTH ATLA
OCE

Anti-Trades or Westerlies   Cape   Horn

Antarctic Circle

PREVAILING WINDS

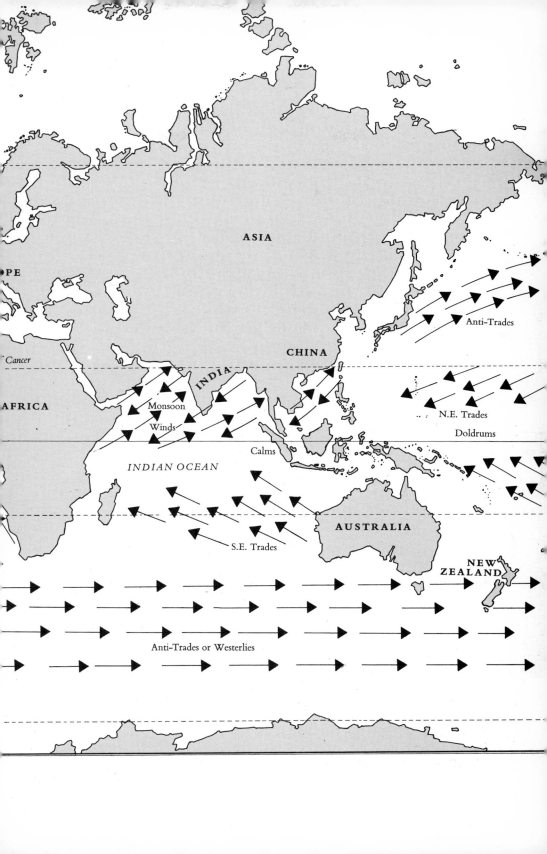

ASIA

Anti-Trades

Cancer

CHINA

INDIA

AFRICA

Monsoon

Winds

N.E. Trades

Calms

Doldrums

INDIAN OCEAN

AUSTRALIA

S.E. Trades

NEW
ZEALAND

Anti-Trades or Westerlies

PE

This photograph dramatizes one of the difficulties of sailing the clippers. The men are standing on the foot-ropes, gathering in the sails because of the coming storm.

American clippers in heavy weather. Owing to the very strong wind the *Meridian* (above) has been stripped almost to 'bare poles'. Only one sail is still set, to steady the ship and prevent excessive rolling. Note the lifeboat which has been torn away from its davits and is trailing in the sea.

On the *Reynard* (right) men are aloft reefing the fore- and mizzen-topsails. The upper sails have already been stowed on their yards.

But on the polar side of each wind system the reverse applies. Winds blow towards the east, inclining towards the poles – in other words south-westerly winds in the northern oceans, north-westerly winds in the southern oceans. And these are called the Anti-Trades.

There are variations, however. The wind systems tend to move north or south with the sun, so that in northern summer, for instance, the trade wind may be found much further to the north than in winter. But then it will die away long before the Equator is reached, whereas in winter it may blow right across the Equator.

Big land masses, too, can upset the system. For instance, in the northern oceans the anti-trades are often erratic because of the continents which partly enclose those oceans. There have been years when the anti-trade in the North Atlantic has completely reversed its direction, and sailing ships have been able to make record passages from Britain to America – right against the usual pattern.

This is unlikely to happen in the far south where there are no land masses. There the anti-trades or westerlies are free to blow right round the world, building up tremendous force and mountainous seas. This was what made the passage round Cape Horn, from east to west against the wind, such a fearsome task for many clipper ships. But it was also this wind which drove the clippers at record speeds from the Cape of Good Hope to Australia. It was on this run that sailors dubbed the westerly wind the Roaring Forties, because it was in the forties of south latitude that it was most felt.

Between the northern and southern wind systems, in the

region of the Equator, lie the Doldrums – hot, humid, dull; a zone of calms and fickle winds, broken by sharp squalls and thunder storms. Sailors might fear Cape Horn, but the Doldrums they hated. It was here that days or weeks might be lost and a fast passage spoilt. It was here that a rival ship might slip ahead with a wind unfelt only a mile away. It was here that the crew had to work night and day, swinging yards and adjusting sails to catch every puff of wind from a dozen different directions. It was here, too, that a sudden squall might take a ship aback, or lay her over on to her beam ends, or rip her sails to pieces and send spars crashing down. Many a tall clipper, having weathered Cape Horn and survived great gales, was reduced almost to a wreck by an unexpected Doldrums squall.

Finally there is the Indian Ocean. Here the enormous land mass of Asia completely dominates the winds. For half the year the land is being heated by the sun and the air is drawn towards it. For the other half the land is cooling and the air flows away from it. This creates a southwest wind in summer, and a northeast wind in winter – the Monsoon winds. And they affect the China Sea as well as the Indian Ocean.

It was every tea-ship captain's hope that he would get his ship loaded and away while the bustling northeast monsoon was still blowing, to give him a straight and fast run down to Java and out into the Indian Ocean. To beat all the way through the reef-strewn China Sea against the southwest monsoon was little short of a nightmare.

*   *   *

The tracks of sailing ships, then, were seldom direct. They followed the winds rather than any straight line. In some cases they were thousands of miles longer than the equivalent steamer tracks. They had to be varied according to the time of year. And in addition every clipper-ship captain had his own ideas on the subject, whatever the sailing directions might say. Where best to cross the Equator, for instance, with a view to getting through the Doldrums quickly, was something about

The *Windhover* (1868), one of the last and best of the British clippers, worked mainly in the Australian trade.

which no two men could agree. And in the China Sea they all had their favourite routes.

There could be little argument about general principles, however. On the North Atlantic, for instance, it was obvious that a clipper running from the United States to Britain should keep well to the north to get the prevailing southwest or westerly anti-trades. But crossing westwards, from Europe to America, she would do well to go south to the latitude of the Azores, pick up the northeast trades, run with them to near the Bahamas, and then turn north with the southwest anti-trades to her port. A wide sweep putting on much extra distance, but with a probability of fine weather and fair winds to shorten the time taken overall.

Going out to China, either from the eastern United States or from Europe, it was usual to follow the trade wind almost across to the coast of Brazil, then to work southward through the Doldrums with the assistance of the powerful Brazil Current which sweeps down that coast. After that, with luck, a short beat through the southeast trades of the South Atlantic should bring the ship into the northwest and west anti-trades, which would carry her across to the Cape of Good Hope and through the southern part of the Indian Ocean to the East Indies.

In the early years, before Maury's recommendations were published, there was a good deal of experimenting with various routes through the East Indies, into or out of the China Sea. Some skippers even tried going right out around Australia! But in later years most clippers used only one route, through the Sunda Strait between Java and Sumatra, and along the coast of Borneo – keeping a good lookout for local pirates and head-hunters as they did so! For the staff of the signal station at Anjer, on Sumatra, the annual appearance of the first clippers racing home was an occasion of great excitement. Encouraging, or discouraging, messages were always signalled to the later ships as to what rivals were ahead of them, and how far in the lead.

57

British clippers homeward bound from China always used the Cape of Good Hope route. Most Americans did, too, but some American captains preferred to go south into the strong westerlies and so past Cape Horn into the Atlantic. This was also the usual route for all clippers, American or British, running home from Australia. Once in the Atlantic a sweep across towards the African coast would bring them into the southeast trades, which would carry them up to the Equator. Thus a voyage to Australia and back, out by way of the Cape of Good Hope, home by way of Cape Horn, was always a voyage round the world.

Following the wind-ways almost always meant long ocean passages far beyond sight of land. The clipper-ship bound for the most distant parts of the world had no ports of call. She never stopped on the way, except in distress. Often her crew would never see land, even in the distance, for three months or more. Not so much as another ship might be sighted in many weeks. It was a lonely life, with nothing but the ship, the sea and sky to look at day after day. Yet some men loved it.

CHAPTER FOUR

The Men of the Clippers

*

THE captain of a clipper was a great man. At sea he was a king, making his own laws, ruling as he saw fit, answerable to none. Ashore he was a most respected citizen, often enough a pillar of the church, owning a fine house, entertaining and being entertained by the leaders of local society in his home port and abroad.

He could indeed be two men – a little god ashore, a very devil at sea. One American skipper, as soon as his ship was clear of harbour and his guests had gone ashore, used to call for a bucket of water to be brought to him on the poop. Then off would come his shore-going top-hat and frock-coat and he would ceremonially wash his face. "I am washing off my shore face," he would tell his awed crew. "Now you behold my sea face." And he would scowl ferociously as he went on to tell his men what they might expect from him if they did not do their duty.

There was one big difference between the crews of British and American clippers. Britain was a seafaring nation and had always possessed a large merchant fleet. Therefore real sailors could always be got fairly easily. There were plenty to go round.

It was quite different in America. America's merchant fleet expanded at a tremendous rate in the 1840s and 1850s, just when the continent was being opened up and the rush to the goldfields was on. Men did not want to go to sea, except perhaps to get to California. To provide crews for the clippers they had to be bribed, coaxed, persuaded, or kidnapped. Lodging-house keepers and others made a business out of providing

Donald Mackay, the great American shipbuilder. He sold four of his famous clippers to James Baines of Liverpool – including the *Donald Mackay* and the *James Baines*.

crews. Men were shipped aboard drunk, drugged, often un-conscious and – so it was said – even dead! No questions were asked. So American captains often found themselves saddled with a crew of foreigners who could not speak English, criminals, wasters and drop-outs of all kinds, with scarcely a real sailor among them.

American skippers and mates acquired a reputation for being able to make a seaman out of anything with two legs. They did it with fist and boot, or with a murderous swinging belaying pin. Some captains never went on deck without a

Captain Anthony Enright was a very successful clipper captain – so successful in fact that James Baines is said to have paid him £1,000 to transfer to the *Lightning*.

loaded pistol, and a shot or two in the general direction of the rigging to hurry men on was not unknown.

But of course this was not universal. We hear most of the extreme cases, of men being beaten to death or kicked out of the rigging, of mutinies and of mates being murdered. There were captains who were true gentlemen, who took their wives to sea with them, who kept at least some of their men for voyage after voyage. Not all American clippers were hell-ships; and there were mutinies on British ships, too.

Shipowners knew that a fast ship was useless without a good captain. Even the *Cutty Sark* made one or two disastrously slow voyages under a captain who was nervous about carrying sail. On the other hand the celebrated American 'Bully' Waterman beat some of the best clippers with a ship which was not a clipper at all – a full-bodied, flat-bottomed New Orleans cotton-carrier named *Natchez*. His run of 78 days from Macao to Boston in 1845 is still a record.

So sometimes owners would bribe a successful man to leave one firm for another. Captain Anthony Enright, who made a name for himself with the early British tea clipper *Chrysolite*, is said to have been paid £1,000 by James Baines to transfer to his big American clipper *Lightning*. It was a great deal of money in those days, when a captain's basic wage might be no more than £20 per month, and was sometimes much less. But clipper captains were usually also paid commissions on their cargoes, bonuses for fast passages, and other extras. Some captains did so well that they became shipowners in their turn, like old John Willis who had the *Cutty Sark* built.

Clipper captains had to earn their money, however. For them life was seldom easy. Record-making passages could only be achieved by constant attention to detail, night and day. Many of the best men scarcely entered their cabins during an entire voyage, sleeping on the chartroom settee and eating when and where they could. Captain Keay of the *Ariel* never slept for more than a few minutes at a time while his ship was in the China Sea, and then it was in a chair on deck. Captain Robertson

Captain John Willis was known as 'Old White Hat'. He did so well as a captain that he later became a shipowner.

of the *Cairngorm*, it was said, never slept except in a chair throughout a homeward voyage. Small wonder that some of them broke down after three or four voyages and had to retire ashore, or go into slower ships.

For the crews life was even harder, except that they had no responsibility to bear. Their pay would be about £4 a month, or less when times were bad. But during the gold-rush boom in America seamen were often bribed with much higher wages – which often they were never paid because they deserted their ships in California and ran off to the diggings.

Usually the seamen were divided into two watches, each watch working four hours, then having four hours off. That went on day and night while the ship was at sea, giving men an average working day of twelve hours, seven days a week. But the cry of "All hands on deck!" was all too frequent, and meant that the watch below had to turn out, even though they had only just come off watch.

Tea clippers carried from twenty to forty seamen, according to size, and according to whether times were good or bad for shipowners. In later years, when economy was all-important, ships far bigger than any clipper had to make do with a dozen seamen and a few boy apprentices. By contrast the old East Indiamen used to employ eighty or a hundred seamen.

Conditions were bad. Out of his little pay a seaman had to provide his own clothes, including oilskins and seaboots, the tools of his trade – knife, sewing gear, etc. – his eating equipment and his bedding, including his mattress, which was a sack filled with straw, known as a 'donkey's breakfast'.

He slept and lived when off duty in the tiny, crowded fo'c'sle in the ship's bows, with the narrow bunks in tiers and the men's own chests for furniture. In bad weather it was often flooded. Bedding and clothing, once wet, could only be dried out when fine weather came, for there was no fire except in the cook's galley. Most sailors eventually suffered from rheumatism and lung ailments. The sea life was not healthy, as landsmen pretended, but was a killer.

The *Kate Carnie*, a British clipper built in 1855, was a small ship
measuring only 600 tons.

Food consisted mainly, as it had done for centuries, of salt meat or fish and dried peas, beans, and hard biscuit. Tinned butter, jam, vegetables and fruit could be had, but little of it found its way into the fo'c'sle. The lack of fresh food containing vitamins still brought on the horrible disease of scurvy, causing gums to swell and teeth to fall out, as it had done for hundreds of years.

Water for drinking was still kept in wooden barrels in many ships, though in some iron tanks were being fitted. Fresh water – though often it was far from fresh! – was rationed at a pint or two a day to each man. Salt water had to be used for all washing purposes, and sometimes even for cooking, which led to skin diseases and sores.

All these matters were improved slightly, however, during the clipper period. In 1854 Britain passed the first Merchant Shipping Act, which laid down rules of employment, including a minimum scale of food. A few years later the issue of lime-juice to combat scurvy was made compulsory in British merchant ships, as it had been for many years in the Royal Navy. American seamen scornfully called British ships 'limejuicers', and British seamen 'limeys'. But in British ships scurvy became a horror of the past.

Worst of all was the way in which a sailor could be cheated of his wages. He was paid only at the end of a voyage. Then, with perhaps a year's money in gold coins jingling at his belt, he would walk straight into 'sailortown' – the close-packed district of drinking shops, gambling houses, dance halls and other disreputable places of entertainment which adjoined the dockside area of every port. Soon he would be drunk, then robbed or swindled of all his money.

Next thing he would find himself in a so-called boarding house run by a 'crimp'. This was a man, or woman, who undertook to find seamen for ships in return for payment in advance of each man's wages for one, two or even three months. Very often even the seaman's clothing would have been stolen from him, so a new outfit would be supplied by the crimp, and the cost, at exorbitant rates, paid by the ship's captain, also of course out of the man's future wages. So off poor Jack would go to sea again, to earn nothing for himself for several months.

This system was at its worst in America, where seamen were in shortest supply. It was in San Francisco that the word 'shanghai-ing' came into being to describe the virtual kidnapping of seamen – and sometimes they were beaten unconscious first – for clippers bound across the Pacific for China tea. In New York some skippers who tried to get men without going to the crimps were themselves beaten-up by hired thugs, or had their ships sabotaged. But most captains worked with the crimps. It was the only way to secure a crew.

In Britain seamen were easier to find and the crimping system was not nearly so vicious. There were some boarding houses to which seamen went year after year, handing over their wages to the proprietor as to a bank and drawing small amounts from him as required. There were some boarding-house keepers who undertook to train young men for their first voyage, though usually such training amounted to no more than teaching them to scrub boards and polish brass!

In any case kidnapping, American style, would have been difficult in Britain after 1854, for the Merchant Shipping Act insisted that all crews be properly signed on in the presence of a government official, the 'shipping master'. Dead, drugged or sandbagged men could scarcely have passed his scrutiny.

Nevertheless even the American system, or lack of system, could have its lighter side. Once, for instance, a gang of rebellious sailors succeeded in shipping away in a clipper the crimp himself, together with a boatload of his thugs. And once, so it is said, a crimp managed to get rid of a detested chief of police of San Francisco by knocking him on the head and sending him off to China.

CHAPTER FIVE

Speed of the Clippers

*

How fast were the clippers? The record day's run of 465 miles by *Champion of the Seas* has already been mentioned. From the *James Baines*, her sister ship, comes one of the most famous log-book entries of all time – 'Ship going 21 knots with main skysail set.' This, it is claimed, is the highest speed ever recorded by a sailing ship.

The big American clippers could achieve much higher maximum speeds than the smaller British ships. This was almost entirely due to their size, not to their design. It is a mathematical fact that the maximum speed at which a ship can be driven through the water depends upon its length. The longer the waterline of the ship, the greater the possible speed. But this does not apply to modern racing dinghies or power boats, which skim over the water rather than drive through it. Clipper ships never skimmed!

Also the bigger the ship, the stouter her masts and spars. A big ship can stand more wind than a smaller one. She can be driven harder. She can make her maximum speed, and hold it, when a smaller ship has to be reefed down for safety.

The great advantage of the British tea clippers was that they could reach their maximum speed in quite a moderate breeze, while the bigger ships would require a whole gale. When the American-built *James Baines* recorded her 21 knots she was storming along in the Roaring Forties with everything set. American clippers frequently carried royals and even skysails around the Horn.

Cutty Sark, probably the fastest of all the tea clippers, never recorded a higher speed than 17 knots. Generally tea clipper

The *Schomberg* was one of the few British clippers that could compare in size with its American cousins. Unluckily she was wrecked on her maiden voyage.

Sovereign of the Seas, one of Donald Mackay's early American masterpieces. In 1852 she was said to be the largest merchant ship in the world – and therefore one of the fastest.

captains were very well satisfied indeed when their ships logged 14 or 15 knots. But because they could make such speeds in quite ordinary weather they often made as good passages, port to port, as their bigger rivals.

James Baines, 2,275 tons, put up a record in 1854 by going out to Australia in 63 days. But in later years *Thermopylae*, only 948 tons, twice went out in 60 days. An American clipper of 1,200 tons, *Witch of the Wave*, rushed tea from China to London in 1852 in 90 days – a record which stood for many years until capped by *Sir Lancelot*, 886 tons, with a run of 89 days. Moreover *Sir Lancelot* had to beat through the China Sea against the southwest monsoon, whereas for *Witch of the Wave* the monsoon had been favourable. It is also worth noting that the record run from China to New York, 78 days, was made by the little *Sea Witch*, 890 tons, in 1848 and was never beaten by any of the later giants.

For much the same reason quite slow steamers scored over clippers on some routes. When *James Baines* achieved her 21 knots the fastest steamers afloat could do only 13 knots all-out. As late as 1888 the Australian mail steamer *Britannia*, approaching Melbourne and making her maximum speed of 16 knots, was overtaken by *Cutty Sark*, nineteen years old but still able to do 17 knots with the right wind. On the North Atlantic famous American clippers like *Red Jacket, Dreadnought* and *Typhoon* often overtook the early Cunard steamers.

But maximum speeds are not everything. A steamer which can *average* 300 miles per day for a whole voyage may easily beat a sailing ship making 400 miles on a few days, but only 100 or so on others. *Red Jacket* and her sisters might *occasionally*

Nightingale, an American clipper, was one of the fastest in the British tea trade in the 1850s. Then she was sold to Brazil and became a slave trader. But she was captured by an American gunboat and was fitted out as a warship in the American Civil War. After those adventures she became a tea clipper once more.

Flying Cloud could boast that she had twice made the journey from New York to San Francisco in 90 days.

cross from New York to Liverpool in 13 days, but sometimes took 21 days or more, whereas by 1860 steamers were regularly making the passage in 12 days and could practically guarantee it.

Record passages are in fact misleading. Ninety days from New York to 'Frisco was a proud boast, but was actually made good only four times in clipper-ship history. *Flying Cloud* did it twice, *Swordfish* and *Andrew Jackson* once each. Far more often the voyage lasted well over a hundred days. Even *Flying Cloud* took 106, 108 and 113 days on three successive voyages.

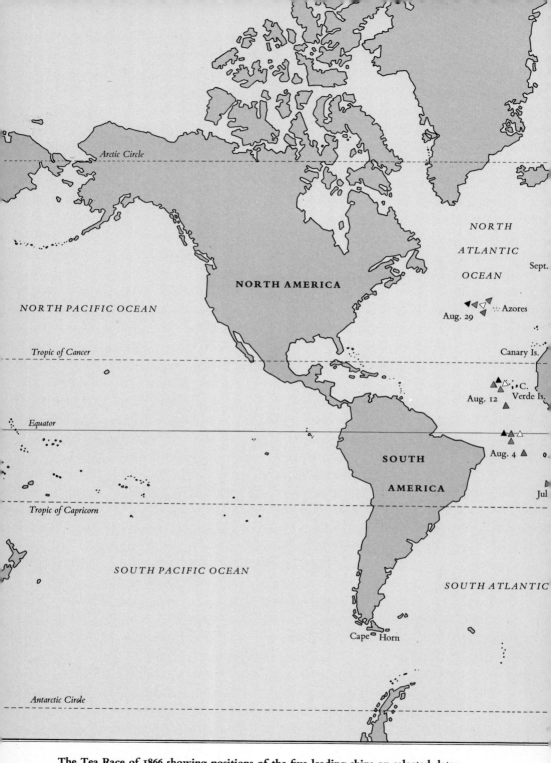

The Tea Race of 1866 showing positions of the five leading ships on selected dates

◀ Ariel ◁ Taeping ◀ Fiery Cross ◀ Serica ◀ Taitsing

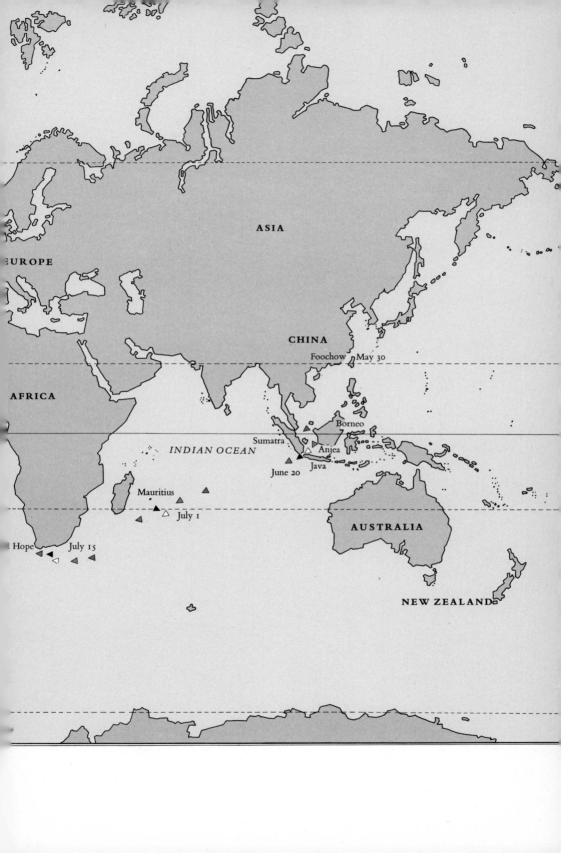

EUROPE

ASIA

CHINA

Foochow May 30

AFRICA

INDIAN OCEAN

Sumatra

Borneo

Anjea

June 20   Java

Mauritius

July 1

AUSTRALIA

Hope   July 15

NEW ZEALAND

Only very occasionally did a tea clipper run from China to Britain in less than 100 days. The fastest ships sometimes took 120 days or more. Even *Cutty Sark* on two voyages took 122 and 127 days respectively. One year, 1857, the American clipper *Celestial* and the British *Lord of the Isles* decided to make a private race of it with heavy bets laid, and both ships took 141 days! Yet in the following year *Lord of the Isles* beat everyone by equalling *Witch of the Wave*'s record run of 90 days.

When a clipper ship sailed there was no saying when she would arrive at her destination. The early steamers were not always reliable, but they were seldom whole months late in arriving.

Some British shipowners engaged in the tea trade tried to compromise by building clippers and giving them auxiliary steam engines for use in calm weather, with screw propellers

Star of Peace was one of the fastest of the colonial clippers. Built in Aberdeen in 1855, she had two consecutive 77-day voyages to Sydney.

Many fine clippers were built in Nova Scotia and New Brunswick. *White Star* was for many years a crack passenger vessel on the Australian run. She was owned by the famous Aberdeen White Star Line.

In 1852, after an incredibly fast passage to and from Australia, the *Marco Polo* was labelled 'The Fastest Ship in the World'. Originally an American clipper, she was sold to James Baines, who fitted her out in red velvet and stained glass for the emigrant trade. On that first voyage she carred nearly 1,000 people.

The *Istamboul*, a clipper fitted with a steam engine.

which could be hoisted clear of the water when not in use. One such was the *Sea King* of 1863. She proved successful in one way, by running home with tea in 78 days – twelve days less than the sailing record. But against that she was far more expensive to run than a true sailing ship, and much of what should have been cargo space was occupied by her engine, boiler and coal. After only one year she was sold to the Confederate States of America for use as a raider in the Civil War, and became famous under her new name of *Shenandoah*, capturing thirty-eight Northern ships.

If only the diesel engine had been invented in 1860, clippers might have competed against steamers for many years longer!

CHAPTER SIX

The Great Tea Race of 1866

*

A T the end of April 1866 the tea clippers were gathering at the anchorage below Foochow on the Min River. Foochow had become the chief loading port on the coast of China, the favourite port for the fastest ships, because here the new season's tea was ready for loading earlier than anywhere else.

Some were fresh out from home with cargoes of cotton cloth and other European goods. Others had been on the coast for a month or two already, filling in time and earning extra freight money by carrying rice from Saigon, Rangoon or Bangkok to Hong Kong, Shanghai, or as far as Yokohama in Japan. For the clippers were working ships and could never remain idle if there was a cargo to be had.

It was hard work and often dangerous work. The China Sea had never at that time been properly surveyed and charted. On his voyage out in the previous December with the brand-new *Ariel*, Captain Keay had found one point in the East Indies placed on the chart eleven whole miles too far west. One island shown on the chart did not exist at all; nor did a reef shown in another place. But elsewhere, instead of the clear open water indicated by the chart, he had found 'a reef very distinct, nearly awash, with many heads of rock showing 10 or 12 feet above water'. For such reasons a clipper captain scarcely dared close his eyes while his ship was in the China Sea.

Nor were the pilots in the various ports at all reliable. Many Chinese, merely promoted fishermen or junk skippers, were apparently quite unable to appreciate that a clipper needed a greater depth of water than a fishing boat. Some were in league with local pirates and were only intent upon trying to run the ship ashore so that she could be stripped by their friends. Other pilots, American or European, were notorious for being more often drunk than sober.

As the ships gathered at Foochow, however, such matters were almost forgotten. Now was the time for preparing the holds for the tea, for overhauling sails and gear ready for the race home, for applying paint and polish so that the ship should not be shamed before her rivals.

Each ship had her distinctive colour scheme or markings. Hulls would be mainly black, sometimes green. *Sir Lancelot*'s masts and spars were pale green, *Ariel*'s pink, others scraped and varnished. The later *Thermopylae* had a green hull, white lower masts and spars, and a lavish amount of gold leaf. But when she entered Foochow with a shining golden cock at her masthead it was too much for other crews to stomach, so they raided her one night and stole it.

Then, about the middle of May when all was ready and only the arrival of the tea was awaited, the crews could take time off to enjoy themselves. Captains and officers would be entertained ashore. But on one day there would be a regatta, with racing by the ships' boats – and sometimes fights between the crews afterwards, just to round off the celebration.

This year, 1866, sixteen of the fastest ships in the world were assembled in the Min River by mid-May. *Ariel*, making her first voyage, was expected to be among the leaders. *Taitsing*, also new, was favoured by some. Among the older ships the crews of *Fiery Cross* and *Serica* had wagered a month's pay against each other. But also in the field were *Taeping, Flying Spur, Black Prince, Chinaman, Falcon, Golden Spur* and half-a-dozen more. Unhappily the beautiful *Sir Lancelot*, also on her maiden voyage, had been plagued by misfortune, including a collision, and was out of the race.

Excitement reached its peak on May 24 when the first

Serica and *Lahloo* at Foochow. *Serica* was one of the contestants in the amazing race of 1866. She docked in London on the same tide as the winning ships *Taeping* and *Ariel*.

THE GREAT SHIP-RACE FROM CHINA TO LONDON.

THE great race between nine of the swiftest clipper sailing-ships in the China trade—competing with each other all the way from Foo-Chow-Foo to London for the premium offered by the London tea importers on the arrival of the first cargo of this season's teas—was decided on Wednesday, the 5th inst., when the Taeping got into London Docks at 9.45 p.m., the Ariel, which came next, getting into the East India Dock half an hour later, and the third ship, the Serica, into the West India Dock at half-past eleven that night.

The following are the names of the nine ships, their owners and commanders, their tonnage, the ports where they were built, and the respective departures from Foo-Chow-Foo:—

Names.	Tonnage.	Captains.	Where Built.	Owners.	Date of Sailing.
Ada	686	Jones ..	Aberdeen	Wade and Co. ..	June 6.
Ariel	853	Keay ..	Greenock	Shaw and Lowther	May 30.
Black Prince ..	750	Inglis ..	Aberdeen	Findlay and Co. ..	June 3.
Chinaman ..	688	Downie ..	Greenock	Park Brothers ..	June 3.
Fiery Cross ..	689	Robinson	Liverpool	J. Campbell	May 29.
Flying Spur ..	731	Ryrie ..	Aberdeen	Robertson and Co.	June 5.
Serica	708	Innes ..	Greenock	Findlay and Co. ..	May 30.
Taeping ..	767	M'Kinnon	Greenock	Roger and Co. ..	May 30.
Taitsing ..	815	Nutsfield	Glasgow	Findlay and Co. ..	May 31.

The struggle, however, was between the Fiery Cross, Ariel, Taeping, and Serica. The Fiery Cross obtained a start of one day over the others. The Serica, Ariel, and Taeping crossed the bar of Foo-Chow-Foo in company together, May 30. The Taitsing started the following day. There was a fair wind (N.E.) blowing, which the Fiery Cross kept to 19·20 N., when they met with a few hours' calm and southerly wind. North-east wind, fresh, again set in, which carried them to the Parcells reef on June 3, though they were not sighted. The Serica, Taeping, and Ariel met with similar weather. The Fiery Cross saw nothing of them until noon of June 7, in lat. 9·37, when she passed a large ship on the opposite tack, believed to have been the Ariel. To the southward of the Parcells they met with strong S.W. winds. As far as we have been enabled to ascertain, the ships passed the lighthouse at Anjer, Strait of Sunda, as follows:—Fiery Cross, at noon of June 18; Ariel, on the morning of June 20; Taeping, on the afternoon of June 20; Serica, at six p.m. of June 22; Taitsing, at ten p.m. of June 22; Black Prince, on June 29.

At this time the Fiery Cross was evidently holding the lead, while the Taitsing, which left Foo-Chow-Foo on the day after the others, had caught up with the Serica, the Fiery Cross heading both by two days. From Anjer they carried good trade winds to the meridian of Madagascar. The Fiery Cross passed Mauritius on June 30, the Ariel on July 2. The Cape of Good Hope was sighted by the Fiery Cross on July 15, at ten p.m. The Ariel rounded the Cape the next day, wind S.E. to E. and N.N.E. The Serica rounded the Cape on the 22nd.

On Aug. 9, in lat. 12·29 N. the Fiery Cross signalled the Taeping, and continued in company till the 17th, with wind variable and light. In lat. 27·53, long. 36·54 W., a fresh breeze sprang up, and took the Taeping out of sight from the Fiery Cross in four or five hours. The Fiery Cross was becalmed, and was not making one knot per hour for twenty-four hours. This circumstance is alleged to have lost her the race. On the 29th she reached lat. 41·5 N., long. 35·51 W., and at ten a.m. of Sept. 6 she sighted the Isle of Wight, it bearing N.N.W., with a wind W.S.W., blowing hard.

At eight o'clock on the morning of Wednesday, the 5th inst., the Ariel and Taeping, which had lost sight of each other for seventy days, found themselves off the Lizard, running neck and neck up the Channel under every stitch of canvas that could be set, with a strong westerly wind. The two ships appear thus in our Illustration, the Taeping in front. During the whole day the two ships kept their position, dashing up the Channel side by side in splendid style, sometimes almost on their beam ends, every sea sweeping their decks. On approaching the pilot station off Dungeness the next morning they each fired blue lights to signalise their position. At daybreak the pilots boarded them at the same moment, and the race was continued in the same exciting manner till they arrived in the Downs, where they both took steam-tugs to tow them to the river. The ships had to shorten sail to enable the tugs to come up and pick up the hawsers to take them in tow. This was about eight o'clock a.m., the tugs starting almost simultaneously, and both ships still neck and neck. The Taeping, however, was fortunate enough to have a superiority in the power of the steam-tug, and reached Gravesend some time before the Ariel. The Serica followed closely upon them. She passed Deal at noon, and got into the river with the same tide which carried the Taeping and Ariel up the river to the docks, when the result of this extraordinary race was declared to be as follows:—

1st. Taeping, docked in London Dock ..	..	9.45 p.m.
2nd. Ariel, docked in East India Dock ..	..	10.15 p.m.
3rd. Serica, docked in West India Dock ..	..	11.30 p.m.

The Taeping, therefore, was the winner of the premium, 10s. per ton extra to be paid to the first sailing-vessel in dock with new teas from Foo-Chow-Foo. The Fiery Cross arrived in the Downs on the 7th, and was compelled to bring up to an anchor on account of a heavy gale blowing, where she remained some time. She, however, managed to get into the London Dock by eight o'clock on Saturday morning, about twenty-eight hours after the Taeping. The fifth ship, Taitsing, arrived in the river some hours after.

The three first ships—the Taeping, Ariel, and Serica—were all built by Messrs. Steele and Co., of Greenock. The Taeping and Ariel were constructed on the composite principle, wood and iron. The Serica is iron built.

The cargoes of the ships were—Taeping, 1,108,709 lb. of tea; Ariel, 1,230,900 lb.; the Serica, 954,236 lb.; Fiery Cross, 854,236 lb; and the Taitsing, 1,093,180 lb.

The time occupied on the voyage by the three ships has been ninety-nine days, being seven days shorter than the time occupied by the Fiery Cross and Serica last year. The Taeping, indeed, though not in the race of last year, made the passage then in five days' less time than they did. Captain Mackinnon, the commander of the Taeping, is a native of the island of Tyree, in Argyleshire, and a Lieutenant in the Royal Naval Reserve.

'The Great Ship-race from China to London', as reported by the *Illustrated London News*, September 22, 1866. The *Serica* was built of wood, not iron as stated in this report.

The Great China Tea Race of 1866 was as close as this picture
suggests. *Taeping* (left) and *Ariel* are shown here racing up the
Channel toward the London docks after a record 99-day run from
Foochow.

lighters loaded with tea came down the river. They went first
to *Ariel*, picked out as favourite by the tea merchants' agents.
Day and night and through a weekend Chinese coolies hustled
the thin wooden tea chests into her, while her mates supervised
the stowage and made all sure and safe. By Monday afternoon,
May 28, her holds were full and she was ready to go. A steam
tug took her down to deep water to anchor for the night. By
five o'clock next morning, with the steam tug in attendance,
she was on her way down river to the sea.

But other ships were not far behind her. *Fiery Cross* had
finished loading during the night and was on *Ariel*'s heels.
Taeping and *Serica* were behind her, and *Taitsing* a few hours
behind them.

Then bad luck hit *Ariel*. Her tug got into difficulties and
collided with her and she had to let go her anchor. Scarcely
had she done so than *Fiery Cross* went past her with another
tug, and jeering sailors lining the rail. So another night was
wasted, and next morning rain and mist brought further delay.
To Captain Keay's disgust *Taeping* and *Serica* now also caught
up with him, and in the end the three ships left the river together, knowing that *Fiery Cross* was already hours ahead
under full sail and racing southward.

That was on May 30. Next day *Taitsing* also got out, and
the race was on. Five ships, reckoned to be the five fastest, had
sailed within thirty hours or so of each other. 14,000 miles of
ocean travel lay ahead of them, with every kind of wind and
weather. Who would win?

The first lap, of 2,500 miles or so through the China Sea to
Java, was easily the worst. The southwest monsoon was fickle,
with the wind sometimes dying away to nothing, sometimes
blasting at the ships in furious squalls, but very seldom in their
favour. Experienced captains kept close to the coast of Indo-
China (Vietnam) using the land and sea breezes which came
each night and morning near the shore. Captain Robinson of
the *Fiery Cross*, as wily as any man in the fleet and knowing
every trick and whim of his six-year-old ship, managed to keep

Black Prince had the distinction of coming last in the Great Race of 1866.

his lead all the way through that difficult first lap. *Fiery Cross* passed the signal station at Anjer at noon on June 18. *Ariel* and *Taeping* followed, five hours apart, 'on June 20. *Serica* went through on June 23 and *Taitsing*, sadly lagging, not until late evening on June 26.

So far the ships had seen little of each other. But the complications of sailing through the China Sea, with every captain having his own choice route, are well illustrated by the fact that on June 8 *Taeping* and *Fiery Cross* had passed in sight of each other, sailing in opposite directions!

Once out into the Indian Ocean there was a different picture, however. Now the southeast trade wind blew steady and strong and the ships could set every stitch of canvas – skysails and watersails, stunsails and flying jibs, and that mysteriously-named sail, the 'Jamie Green', along the bowsprit below the headsails. Now the ships could really sail, and every man on board could feel the thrill of racing.

But still *Fiery Cross* kept ahead. She passed south of Mauritius, 3,000 miles from Anjer, on June 29, still with *Ariel* and *Taeping* two days astern, still with *Serica* three days behind them and *Taitsing* trailing in the rear.

Then once again luck took a hand. The trade wind died away. Captain Robinson took the *Fiery Cross* over to the coast of Natal to catch the south-sweeping Agulhas Current, but by doing so missed the wind. *Ariel* and *Taeping*, keeping further south, found good easterly winds and caught up on her. *Serica* went even further south, missed the easterly wind and ran into the westerlies, and so was set back. *Taitsing* was still trailing at the Cape of Good Hope, nine days behind the leader.

Luck, good and bad, went with the ships through the South Atlantic. *Fiery Cross* and *Ariel*, not far apart now, took a direct course towards St Helena and were frustrated by light winds. *Taeping* and *Serica*, keeping nearer the African coast, had stronger winds and made up time. In fact *Taeping* ran right ahead of even *Fiery Cross* and sighted St Helena first, on July 27.

Serica could not quite catch *Fiery Cross*, but did manage to get ahead of *Ariel*.

At Ascension *Taeping* was still leading the fleet, with *Fiery Cross* second. But *Ariel* had recovered third place from *Serica* and was hard on the heels of *Fiery Cross*. *Taitsing*, too, was beginning to creep up from her tail position. And so the order remained as they crossed the Equator, with *Taeping*, *Fiery Cross* and *Ariel* practically neck and neck, *Serica* two days behind and *Taitsing* still far astern but showing signs of catching up.

And then came Doldrum weather, which that year extended far into north latitudes. *Taeping* and *Fiery Cross* were in sight of each other for a few days, till *Taeping* found a wind and went ahead, leaving a furious Captain Robinson in the *Fiery Cross* utterly becalmed for a whole day. Nor did either captain know that, only just out of sight beyond the horizon, *Ariel* was going ahead of both their ships. Nor, for that matter, that *Serica* was very close behind or that *Taitsing* had clipped two clear days off her rivals' lead.

Now the breeze came more steadily and the ships began to race for the Azores. On August 29 *Ariel*, *Fiery Cross*, *Taeping* and *Serica* all passed Flores within hours of each other – *Fiery Cross* having gone ahead of *Taeping* once more. And then, astonishingly, *Taitsing* came racing along only two days, instead of a whole week or more, behind the rest.

Nearing home latitudes the weather became brisk, with west and southwest gales. On drove the clippers, making the most of it, with lookouts aloft straining their eyes for sight of land and for the topsails of their competitors.

Soon after midnight on September 5 the crew of *Ariel* cheered as the light on Bishop Rock in the Scilly Isles came into view. But at daybreak they held their breath and wondered. Away to starboard they could see another clipper tearing along with everything set. Captain Keay took one look through his glass and knew that it was *Taeping*.

Neck and neck they raced up the Channel, a wonderful sight, both ships making fourteen knots and the sea creaming away from their bows. Past the Lizard and Start Point and Portland they went, with sometimes one ship a few yards ahead, sometimes the other. Neither ship would reduce sail by so much as a handkerchief until they were past the Isle of Wight, then both ships took in their Jamie Greens together so that their crews could clear the anchors for lowering.

At midnight the two ships swept past Beachy Head. In the early hours of the morning they were both off Dungeness, signalling for pilots. *Ariel* edged in towards the pilot cutter. *Taeping* tried to get past her, but Captain Keay swung *Ariel* round and blocked the way. At six o'clock *Ariel* got her pilot aboard and dashed away, gaining a mile over *Taeping* before that ship could follow. *Ariel* was still leading when, off Deal, the sailing came to an end and both ships took steam tugs.

The sailing was ended, but not the race. And now *Taeping* scored, getting a much more powerful tug. As she entered the Thames she went well ahead and at Gravesend led *Ariel* by nearly an hour. But then she had to anchor to await the tide and *Ariel* caught up with her.

At nine o'clock next morning *Ariel* was off the East India Dock where she was to berth. But she was drawing too much water to get in and had to wait for the night tide. *Taeping* went on to the London docks, reached them at ten that night, went straight in and got a rope ashore just twenty minutes before *Ariel* managed it. Twenty minutes apart, after 14,000 miles and 100 days! No wonder the two captains, M'Kinnon of *Taeping* and Keay of *Ariel*, agreed to share the prize and bonus awarded by the tea merchants for the first ship home.

Nor was that the end of this amazing race. Only four hours after *Ariel* and *Taeping* had shed their canvas off Deal, *Serica* did the same. In fact she docked in London on the same tide as the other two ships. Then next night *Fiery Cross* came in, her captain furious at having had to anchor at the mouth of the Thames because of a roaring gale. And no sooner had she docked than the laggard *Taitsing*, having caught up marvel-lously, came steaming up the river behind her tug.

Five ships had sailed almost together, and three months and a few days later had docked almost together. There had never been such a close-fought tea race before, nor was there ever again.

Table of Comparative Measurements of Selected Ships

Name	Type	Year Built	Tons
Princess Amelia	East Indiaman	1815	1250
Falcon	Opium clipper	1824	351
Ellenborough	Blackwall frigate	1842	926
Rainbow	American clipper	1845	750
Sea Witch	,, ,,	1846	907
Oriental	,, ,,	1849	1003
Stornoway	British tea clipper	1850	506
Chrysolite	,, ,, ,,	1851	471
Witch of the Wave	American clipper	1851	1498
Flying Cloud	,, ,,	1851	1793
Challenge	,, ,,	1851	2006
Challenger	British tea clipper	1852	699
Cairngorm	,, ,, ,,	1853	938
Lord of the Isles	,, ,, ,,	1853	770
Great Republic	American clipper	1853	4555
Lightning	American-built British-owned emigrant clipper	1854	1462
Champion of the Seas	,, ,, ,,	1854	1947
James Baines	,, ,, ,,	1854	2275
Donald Mackay	,, ,, ,,	1855	2408
Fiery Cross	British tea clipper	1860	695
Malabar	Blackwall frigate	1860	1219
Alabama	Steam frigate	1861	1040
Taeping	British tea clipper	1863	767
Serica	,, ,, ,,	1863	708
Sea King	Auxiliary steam clipper	1863	1018
Ariel	British tea clipper	1865	853
Sir Lancelot	,, ,, ,,	1865	886
Taitsing	,, ,, ,,	1865	815
Titania	,, ,, ,,	1866	879
Thermopylae	,, ,, ,,	1868	991
Cutty Sark	,, ,, ,,	1869	963
Torrens	British wool and emigrant clipper	1875	1335
Thomas W. Lawson	American seven-masted steel schooner	1902	5218

Length feet	Breadth feet	Depth feet	Remarks
165	42	17	
110	26·4	17	Built as a private yacht
159·6	34·5	23	
154	31·5		The first true clipper. Vanished at sea 1848
170	34	19	Wrecked 1856
185	36	21	First American ship to bring tea to U.K.
158	29	18	First British tea clipper
149	26	17	
220	40	21	
225	41	21·5	Burnt 1873
230·6	43·6	27·6	Wrecked about 1868
174	32	20	
185	36·5	20	
191	28	18·5	The only iron clipper before 1870
325	53		The largest clipper ever built
244	44	23	Burnt 1869
252	45·5	29	Foundered 1877
226	44·8	29	Burnt 1858
266	46·3	29·5	Ended life as coal hulk at Madeira
185	31·7	19·2	Broken up about 1900
207	36·6	22·5	
220	32	17	The Confederate raider. Sunk 1864
183·7	31·1	19·9	Wrecked 1873
186	31	19·5	Wrecked 1873
220	32·5	20·5	Became Confederate raider *Shenandoah*
197·4	33·9	19·6	Vanished at sea 1872
197·5	33·6	21	Foundered 1895
192	31·5	20	
200	36	21	Broken up 1910
212	36	21	Sunk 1907
212·5	36	21	Preserved at Greenwich, London
221	38	21·5	Author Joseph Conrad was once first mate of her
395	50	35·2	Probably the largest sailing vessel ever built. Capsized and lost 1907

Books for further reading

*

The best author on the subject of clipper ships is the late Basil Lubbock, who made a lifelong study of them and knew some of the men who sailed them. His books are full of facts and figures and interesting stories, illustrated with scores of drawings and photographs. They are

THE CHINA CLIPPERS – British and American ships in the tea trade, with details of the annual races.

THE COLONIAL CLIPPERS – about ships in the Australian trade, the gold rush, emigrant and wool clippers.

THE BLACKWALL FRIGATES – with quite a lot about the old East Indiamen.

THE OPIUM CLIPPERS

THE WESTERN OCEAN PACKETS – and clippers on the Atlantic.

THE LOG OF THE 'CUTTY SARK'

All these books are published by Brown, Son and Ferguson of Glasgow, who also publish detailed plans of some of the famous clippers and books to help model makers.

For more information about the East India Company and East Indiamen, see

THE OLD EAST INDIAMEN, by E. Keble Chatterton.

EAST INDIAMEN, THE EAST INDIA COMPANY'S MARITIME SERVICE, by Sir Evan Cotton.

JOHN COMPANY AT WORK, by Holden Furber.

One of Captain Marryat's famous sea-adventure novels, *Newton Forster*, describes life aboard an East Indiaman.

A novel dealing with life aboard a China clipper, and the tea racing, is *Bird of Dawning*, by John Masefield. A lot of John Masefield's poetry also describes life aboard sailing ships, especially his long poem *Dauber*. John Masefield, who became Poet Laureate in 1930, served in sailing ships as a young man.

Another famous writer with first-hand experience of sailing ships is Joseph Conrad. He was at one time first mate in the clipper *Torrens*, in the Australian trade. Read his *Mirror of the Sea*, *Nigger of the Narcissus* and other stories.

Two Years Before the Mast by Richard Dana has already been mentioned. It is a splendid story of a voyage round Cape Horn to California just before the days of the clippers.

Herman Melville, author of *Moby Dick*, was also a sailor in the early clipper period. Read his *Redburn* and *White Jacket*.

The publishers are grateful to the National Maritime Museum, London, for the use of the photographs in this book. Pictures not provided by the museum are from the following sources: page 16, The Ceylon Tea Centre; page 18, George White Sanderson & Co. Ltd.; page 36, The Mansell Collection; page 47, Radio Times Hulton Picture Library.

Picture Research by Margaret Johnson

Index

*